THE CAVE OF SHADOWS

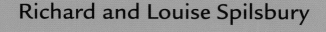
Explore light and use science to survive

Richard and Louise Spilsbury

Smart Apple Media

Published by Smart Apple Media, an imprint of Black Rabbit Books
P.O. Box 3263, Mankato, Minnesota 56002
www.smartapplemedia.com

Published by arrangement with Watts Publishing, London.

Cataloging-in-Publication Data is available from the Library of Congress
ISBN: 978-1-62588-147-2   (library binding)
ISBN: 978-1-62588-395-7   (paperback)
ISBN: 978-1-62588-578-4   (eBook)

Printed in the United States by CG Book Printers
North Mankato, Minnesota

PO 1723
3-2015

Photo Credits
Dreamstime: Anton Petuhkov, Berean, Sifis Diamantidis, Sylwia Nowik, Tetyana Kysyonz; Shutterstock: Ales Liska, andreiuc88, Andre Nantel, Archiwiz, basel101568, Devochka i zaicheg, dramaj, Dziurek, elsyl, fotofundi, fototehnik, Galyana Andrushko, geographio, jeff gynane, Kurt Kleeman, malko, nubephoto, Potapov Alexander, romawka, RUI FERREIRA, Sergemi, spline_x.

Bold words in the text are included in the glossary

WHO'S WHO?

JESS

Jess is a bit of a daredevil. She's always first to try something new. She loves skateboarding, climbing, and adventure stories.

BEN

Ben is a bit of a gadget fanatic. He carries his backpack with him at all times and it's full of useful—and not so useful—stuff.

AMELIE

Amelie is a science whiz. She's not a know-it-all, but she often has the right answers. She doesn't like getting her clothes dirty or her hair messed up.

ZAC

Zac is the youngest and although he never wants to be left out, he can get a bit nervous and is easily spooked.

CONTENTS

INTO THE DARK

"He-e-e-lp!" shouts Jess. "Come quickly! Poppy's chased a rat into this cave."

"I told you not to bring that puppy with us!" snaps Amelie.

"Well, I'm not going into that dark, scary cave after her. Let's wait till she comes out," says Zac.

"She could get hurt or lost! Come on, we'll see all right once our eyes get used to the dark," pleads Jess.

"No," says Amelie. "Without light we won't be able to see where we're going, and it could be dangerous."

A loud yelp comes from inside the cave and the three friends look at each other in panic. Just then, Ben runs up— with his bulging backpack on his back, as usual.

"It's okay," Ben says quickly. "I've got a flashlight and a headlamp. Let's go."

"I've got a bad feeling about this..." warns Zac, following the others into the dark.

WHAT DO YOU THINK?

Is Amelie right? If there is no light, can you see?

Test how light helps us to see.
You need:

- bag made from thick, tightly woven material
- a few small objects such as a ball, a pencil, a spoon (nothing sharp)
- small flashlight (not too strong a light)

1

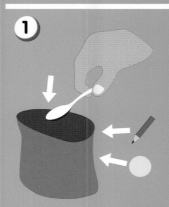

Put a few small objects into your bag.

2

Rest the bag on the table, and look into it. Hold the top edge tightly around your eyes, so that no light can get in from outside. What do you see?

3

Turn on the flashlight and hold it so that it points into the bag. What do you see? Turn off the flashlight so that it no longer gives out light. What happens now?

WHY IT WORKS

Amelie is right, we need light in order to see. We see some objects because they are luminous (they give off their own light), such as the Sun or a flashlight. We see other objects when light shines on them and bounces into our eyes. That's why we can only see the objects in the bag when the light from the flashlight bounces off them and back to our eyes.

WE'RE NOT ALONE

"Good job you had those flashlights in your bag, Ben," says Zac. "It's so dark in here we really wouldn't be able to see a thing without them."

"Wait!" whispers Jess urgently, holding her hand up in warning to the others. "I think there's someone or something else down here..."

"There can't be," says Amelie. "Poppy would have barked at them. Keep moving—it's really cramped here."

"Hang on," says Ben. "Shine your flashlight ahead again."

"No! What if it sees us?" hisses Zac. "Then we'll all be in real trouble."

"I don't think so," laughs Ben. "Jess, you were scared by your own **reflection** in that pile of scrap metal over there!"

"Well, how come there aren't reflections of me all over the walls, too?" retorts Jess, a little embarrassed. "And what kind of idiot dumps their garbage like that?"

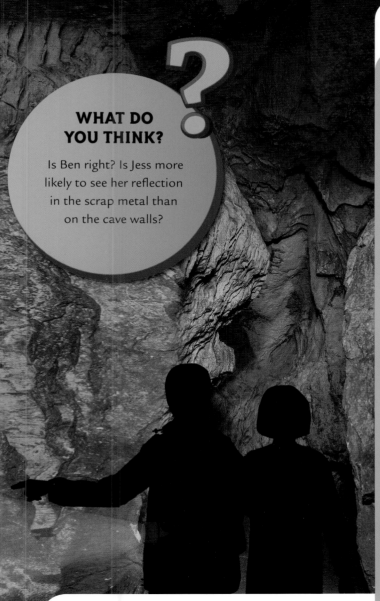

WHAT DO YOU THINK?

Is Ben right? Is Jess more likely to see her reflection in the scrap metal than on the cave walls?

WHY IT WORKS

When light bounces off an object, it is called reflection. Different surfaces reflect light differently. When light hits a very smooth and shiny surface, such as a mirror, it reflects at a matching **angle**—like a ball bouncing off the ground. When it hits a surface that is rough, the light bounces off in all sorts of directions so no clear image can be seen. This is like bouncing a ball on very uneven ground. There are some surfaces from which light does not bounce back at all, and no reflection is seen.

PROVE IT!

Test how different surfaces reflect light. You need:

- scissors ● ruler ● piece of tagboard
- modeling clay ● flashlight ● white paper
- fabric ● sandpaper ● small mirror
- crinkly aluminium foil

1
Ask an adult to help you cut a thin slot about 2 inches (5 cm) long in the middle of one of the edges of the tagboard. Use the modeling clay to stand the card upright on a table, with the slot at the bottom.

2
Close the curtains or turn off the light so the room is a bit darker. Lie the flashlight on the table so it shines through the slot in the tagboard. One at a time, hold the paper, fabric, sandpaper, and crinkly aluminium foil in the narrow beam of light coming through the slit. What do you notice?

3
Now hold a mirror in the beam of light. What do you notice?

THE LONG TUNNEL

"Hurry up!" snaps Jess. "I can hear Poppy barking up ahead, she might be hurt."

"I can't go any faster," says Amelie. "It's too dark back here."

"Aaa-aa-r-g-h!!" screams Zac. "I've fallen and something's got me by the foot. Get it off. Get it off!"

"Hang on," says Ben, shining his flashlight at Zac. "You haven't been grabbed by a hungry cave monster—your foot is just trapped between two rocks!"

"Well I can't see where I'm going because you two are hogging the flashlights," complains Zac.

"It's not our fault," protest Jess and Ben together. "Light travels in a straight line."

"Yeah, that's a likely story," mutters Zac.

WHAT DO
YOU THINK?

Are Jess and Ben right?
Does light travel in
a straight line?

PROVE IT!

Test how light moves.
You need:

- four pieces of tagboard (all the same size)
- torch ● pencil ● ruler
- drinking straw ● modeling clay

1

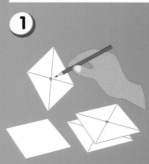

Draw a cross on three of the tagboard by laying a ruler from one corner to the other across both diagonals. Use the pointy end of the pencil to make a hole in the middle of each of these three tagboard pieces (where the X meets in the middle). Wiggle the pencil around a bit to make the hole big enough to poke the straw through.

2

Use the straw to line up the three holes in the tagboard. Then use modeling clay to hold the pieces in position on the table, with the holes lined up. Remove the straw. Use modeling clay to stand the fourth tagboard piece (with no hole) behind the third card. Shine a flashlight through the hole in the first card. What happens?

WHY IT WORKS

Jess and Ben are right. Light is a form of **energy** that travels in straight lines called **rays** from light **sources**. When the three holes in the tagboard are lined up, the light travels through the holes. If the middle piece is moved to one side so that the holes are not lined up, the light ray doesn't pass through the hole in the middle one. It travels in a straight line and hits the middle one to the side of the hole.

3

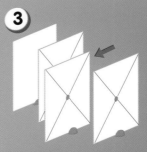

Now move the second piece in the row and reattach it to the table so that it doesn't line up with the others. Shine a flashlight through the hole in the first one. What happens?

SEEING SPOOKS

"Come on, Zac," says Amelie. "We're going to fall behind the others."

"I'm not going another step," whispers Zac, pointing with a shaking finger at a large pale shape glowing in the tunnel ahead of them.

"It lo-loo-looks like some sort of cave ghost!" splutters Amelie. "What do we do?"

"Let me think... stand here and tremble? Or cry?" suggests Zac.

"Hang on a minute," sighs Amelie. "I know what it is now—it's just a **column** of **translucent** rock! It looks like it's glowing because only some of the light from Ben's flashlight is going through it. Phew!"

WHAT DO YOU THINK?

Is Amelie right? Do some things let some, but not all, light through?

PROVE IT!

Build a tester tube to find out what can happen when light hits different objects.
You need:

- six cardboard tubes
- scissors
- six elastic bands
- six different materials, such as plastic wrap, wax paper, plastic shopping bag, aluminium foil, white paper, colored paper, fabric

1

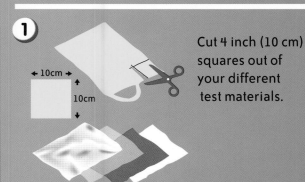

Cut 4 inch (10 cm) squares out of your different test materials.

←10cm→
10cm

2 Wrap one square of material around one end of each cardboard tube. Hold each square in place with an elastic band.

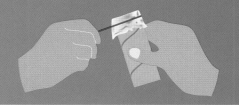

3 Take turns holding the open end of each tester tube to your eye, and point the other end at a window or light and look through it. (Don't point your tester tube up towards the Sun or a very bright light, as this could hurt your eye.) How much light gets through?

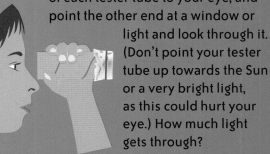

WHY IT WORKS

When light hits a material, three things can happen. If the material is **transparent**, like clear flat glass, light passes through it easily and we can see clearly through it. If the material is translucent, like a net curtain, it lets some light through but we cannot see clearly through it. Compare a bathroom window to the ones in your classroom. How are they different? If the materal is **opaque**, like wood, it blocks light completely so we can't see through it at all.

MONSTER OF THE CAVE?

"Now what?!" snaps Jess. "Why are you pulling at my sleeve, Zac?"

"Keep still. I think there's a giant bat up ahead of us."

"A bat?" screams Jess. "No, I hate those things! It'll get tangled in my hair and suck my blood!"

"Those are just silly stories," says Ben crossly. "Bats are too clever at finding their way in darkness to get tangled in anything. And they eat fruit or insects, not people—even if your blood would taste sweet from all the candy you eat!"

"Cool it, all of you! It's just a **shadow** from a moth on the front of Ben's flashlight." says Amelie.

"What, the biggest moth of all time?! I'm not waiting to find out if you're right this time," says Jess, unconvinced. "Let's run—we still haven't found Poppy!"

WHAT DO YOU THINK?

Is Amelie right? Can a small object make a big shadow?

PROVE IT!

Test how light makes large and small shadows.
You need:

- flashlight with a strong light **beam**
- darkened room
- three small objects for making shadows, such as a comb, feather, and toy dinosaur

①

Lie the flashlight on a table so that it shines towards a wall. Place one of your test objects in the line of light from the flashlight, near the wall. Try the other test objects in the same position. What kind of shadow do they make?

②

Now hold your test objects in the line of light from the flashlight but nearer the flashlight, one at a time. What do you notice? How big a shadow can you make with the small objects?

WHY IT WORKS

Amelie is right. A small object can make a big shadow. A shadow is formed when rays of light are blocked by an opaque object, creating darkness behind the object. That's why a shadow has the same shape as the object in front of it. Objects close to a light source block a lot of light, so they make big, fuzzy shadows. Objects further from a light source block a little light, so they make small, clear shadows.

GLINTING IN THE DARK

"What are you doing?" cries Ben, grabbing Jess to stop her reaching into a pool of water.

"Let go! I'm trying to get that thing **shimmering** in the water. If it's Poppy's name tag, we'll know she went this way and not down the other tunnel."

"But the water might be deeper than it looks, and you could fall in."

"Don't be silly," says Jess crossly. "I've got great eyesight—I can see how deep it is."

WHAT DO YOU THINK?

Is Ben right? Can water make objects appear closer than they really are?

16

PROVE IT!

Try this water trick.
You need:

● coin ● mug ● jug of water

1 Place the empty mug on a table and drop a coin into it. Look over the rim of the mug so that you can see the coin, and then move the mug slowly away from you until the coin just disappears from sight.

2 Keep your head still, and with one hand slowly pour water into the mug. Does the coin come back into sight?

WHY IT WORKS

Ben is right. Water bends light, so when you look at objects under the water they can appear closer than they really are. This happens because light travels at different **speeds** through different **materials**. Light slows down when it moves from air to water, and as it slows down it changes its **direction**. This bending of light is called **refraction**.

"OK, you were right," admits Jess. "The water was deeper than it looked, and you had to hold my legs so I could reach into it safely."

"Yeah, but you were right, too," says Ben kindly. "It was Poppy's name tag, so we know we're on the right trail!"

FINDING TREASURE

"Yikes!" shouts Amelie with disgust. "A huge rat just ran across my feet into that hole!"

"A rat?!" shrieks Zac, leaping into Jess's arms. "Are there more of them?"

"No," says Jess, trying to drop Zac to the floor as he holds on tight.

"Maybe Poppy went through that hole, too," says Ben, crouching down. "Wow! There are colored gems in here. I could buy some great new gadgets if we can get them out!"

"Sorry to disappoint you, but those are just worthless rock **crystals**. They're acting like a **prism** and splitting your flashlight into different colors," explains Amelie.

"Can you say that again in English, please?" asks Ben, looking confused.

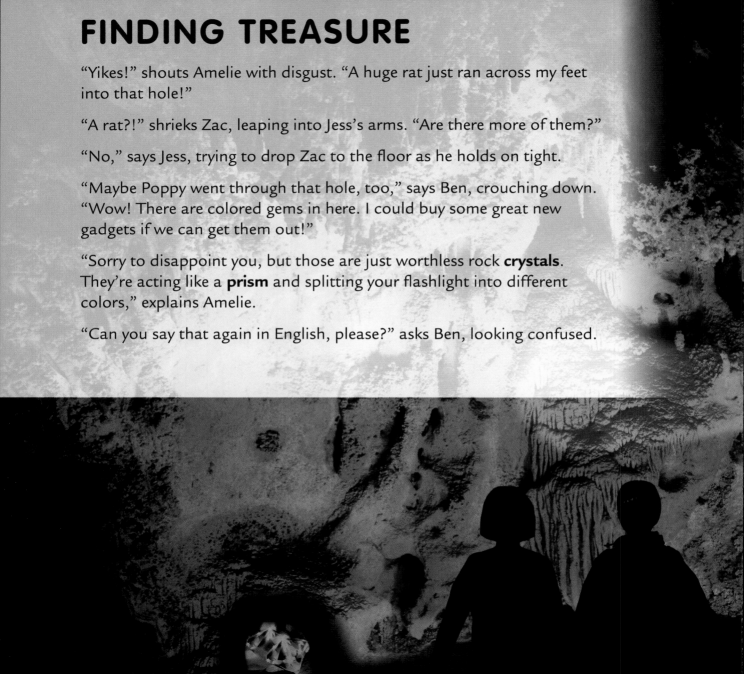

PROVE IT!

See if you can separate light into different colors.
You need:

- tagboard ● scissors ● shallow baking tray
- water ● modeling clay ● small mirror ● ruler
- window with sunshine coming through it

1  Cut a 4 inch (10 cm) long, wide slit into the long edge of the tagboard, a couple inches in from the edge.

2 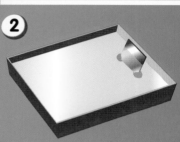 Put about 1 inch (2.5 cm) of water in the bottom of the baking tray. Then rest the small mirror in the tray at an angle, with the top edge resting against the side of the tray. Use blobs of modeling clay to hold the mirror in place.

3  Place the water tray in front of a sunny window, with the mirror facing the window. Hold the tagboard so that light shines through the slit onto the part of the mirror under the water. Keep moving it until the mirror reflects light back onto the tagboard. What can you see?

WHY IT WORKS

You have made a water prism. A prism is something that can split light into its separate colors. Amelie is right. Light seems colorless but it is really a mixture of colors. We can see the colors of light when it shines through a prism of glass or crystal. When light shines through drops of rainwater, we sometimes see a rainbow.

WHAT DO YOU THINK?

Is Amelie right? Can light be split up into different colors?

HIDDEN SPACES

"Now what?" groans Jess. "Poppy is small enough to get through that gap, but we're not. How can we check if she went that way?"

"Zac's got a small head. Perhaps he could poke it through the hole," suggests Amelie helpfully.

"Aren't you funny!" says Zac. "My head may be on the small side, but my brain is big enough to know that I'd get stuck trying that."

"Backpack to the rescue!" shouts Ben. "I've got all we need to make a periscope—lucky you guys drank all the juice and left me with the cartons! I'll turn on this glowstick first, and then use a periscope to bend the light and see what's in there."

WHAT DO YOU THINK?

Is Ben right? Can a periscope help you see what's on the other side of a solid wall?

PROVE IT!

Try making this simple periscope.
You need:

● two empty one-quart (one-liter) rectangular milk or juice cartons
● double-sided sticky tape
● two mirrors that fit into the cartons ● tagboard ● scissors

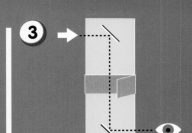

1 window

Open the top of one carton and the bottom of the other. Tape the open parts together to make one long box. Now ask an adult to help you cut two windows out of the box—one on each side. One window should be at the top of the box's front side, and the other should be at the bottom of its back side.

2
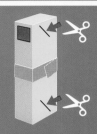

Ask an adult to help you make diagonal (45-degree angle) slits in the top and bottom of each of the wider sides of the carton. The slits must be at the same angle and position on each side of the carton, in the middle of the sides.

Use double-sided sticky tape to stick each mirror to a piece of tagboard that will slide through the slits. The reflective sides of the mirrors should face towards the two windows. Look through the bottom window. You should be able to see out of the top window. If you can't, adjust the mirrors until you can. Then try looking around a corner with your periscope!

WHY IT WORKS

Ben's right. A periscope uses mirrors to change the direction of light and help you see around solid objects. Light reflects away from a mirror at the same angle that it hits a mirror. In a periscope, two mirrors are angled so that light from outside hits the top mirror and reflects to the bottom mirror. This light reflects into your eye, so you can see the image from the top mirror.

FOUND BUT LOST!

"Poppy! There you are!" cries Jess, scooping the excited puppy into her arms. "I told you guys I heard her whining down that tunnel and not in that stupid hole! Look—she's hurt her paw..."

"Well, that's another reason—besides the rats—to get out of here quickly," says Zac. "But how? We're totally lost, aren't we?"

"Maybe not..." says Ben. "There's some words scratched onto this rock. They might tell us how to get out of the cave!"

"The writing is tiny, though. Even up close, it's too small to read properly," says Amelie, squinting at the words.

"Ben—have you got an old water bottle in your backpack?" asks Jess suddenly. "I could use some curved plastic from it to make a **lens** that'll help us read it!"

WHAT DO YOU THINK?

Is Jess right? Can curved lenses help us see things better?

PROVE IT!

Make and test your own **magnifying** lens.
You need:

- empty 64 ounce (two-liter) bottle ● water ● scissors
- marker ● book or newspaper

1

Use the marker to draw a circle at the top of the bottle.

2

Ask an adult to help you cut out the circle. Then lie it on the table so it makes a bowl shape, and put a large drop of water in the middle of the disc.

3

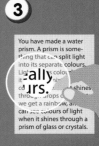

You have made a water prism. A prism is some- thing that can split light into its separate colours. Light is colou... it ... c... shines throug... drops ... we get a rainbow, a... can see colours of light when it shines through a prism of glass or crystals.

Hold your magnifying lens over the words in a book to see if it works.

WHY IT WORKS

Jess is right. Lenses are curved pieces of transparent plastic or glass that refract, or bend, light. Magnifying lenses use **convex** lenses, which have at least one curved surface and are thicker in the middle than at the sides. Your plastic bottle lens and the top of the water drop both curve outwards, so you have created a double convex lens. When you hold the lens close to a page, it bends and widens the light rays before they reach your eyes, making the words appear larger.

INTO THE LIGHT

"We made it! I thought we were never going to get out of there..." says Jess. "Good job—the magnifying lens worked and the writing told us which way to go. It was pretty confusing even with the directions."

"Ow!" cries Ben suddenly. "After so long in the dark, it hurts my eyes to go into the bright sunlight."

"Me too," say Zac and Amelie together, shielding their eyes with their hands.

"But we need to get Poppy home fast to clean her paw and see if it's okay," says Jess.

"Well, you might not believe it but I can solve this problem!" says Zac proudly. "I did a project on **Inuit** people recently. They wore **goggles** with slits in to protect their eyes from the sunlight **glaring** off the snow. If Ben's got duct tape in his backpack I can make us some."

"What does Ben not have in that backpack?" laughs Amelie. "Let's make them and get home!"

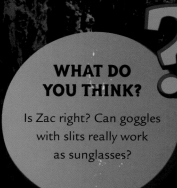

WHAT DO YOU THINK?

Is Zac right? Can goggles with slits really work as sunglasses?

24

PROVE IT!

Make your own goggles.
You need:

- string ● scissors ● duct tape (or other wide tape)
- paper clip ● marker

1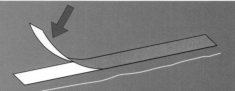

Wrap a piece of string around your head at forehead level, and cut one end where the string meets. Then cut two pieces of duct tape just a bit longer than the string and stick the two sticky sides of the pieces together. Line the two sides up carefully before sticking them together because they are tough to pull apart again!

2

Bend the duct tape strip into a circle, and clip the two ends together with the paper clip. Put this mask on over your eyes. Use the marker to very gently draw a line where your eyes are.

3

Take the mask off and cut lines where the marker lines are, to make two slits. When you put the goggles back on, make sure they fit close to your face to prevent light getting through.

WHY IT WORKS

When light shines into your eyes, it hits a part called the **retina** at the back of each eye. The retina sends messages about what your eyes see to the brain. Bright sunlight can damage retinas. These sunglasses let in enough light for your eyes to see, but the opaque material stops too much sunlight entering and hurting your eyes.

QUIZ

1 Objects that give off their own light are called:

a) luminous

b) reflective

c) transparent

2 When light bounces back off an object or surface, this is called:

a) bending

b) absorption

c) reflection

3 How do you see the words on this page?

a) Light reflects off the book and enters your eyes.

b) Light reflects off your eyes and enters the book.

c) Light comes from your eyes and reflects off the book.

4 Which of these three surfaces reflect the most light?

a) rough and dull

b) smooth and shiny

c) smooth and dull

5 Which of these statements are true?

a) Light travels in straight lines.

b) Light travels through any material.

c) Light is a form of energy.

6 Match each word with its meaning.

a) transparent

b) translucent

c) opaque

1) lets some light through but we cannot see clearly through it

2) blocks light completely so we can't see through it at all

3) light passes through it easily and we can see clearly through it

7b | 8b | 9a | 10b | 11a | 12c How did you do?

7 **When do shadows occur?**

a) When light reflects off a shiny surface.

b) When an opaque object blocks the path of light.

c) When light travels through an object.

8 **When light bends as it passes through water we say it...**

a) reflects

b) refracts

c) bounces

10 **When light hits a mirror, does it...**

a) get absorbed by the mirror?

b) reflect away at the same angle that it hits the mirror?

c) reflect away at many different angles from the mirror?

9 **What does a prism do?**

a) It splits light into its separate colors.

b) It gives off light.

c) It creates shadows.

12 **Which part of the eye can be damaged by sunlight?**

a) eyelashes

b) eyebrows

c) retina

11 **What are lenses?**

a) curved pieces of transparent plastic or glass that refract light

b) curved pieces of opaque plastic or glass that refract light

c) curved pieces of transparent plastic or glass that absorb light

FIND OUT MORE

BOOKS

Experiments with Sound and Light (Excellent Science Experiments)
Chris Oxlade, Rosen Publishing, 2015

Hands-on Science: Sound and Light
Sarah Angliss, Kingfisher, 2013

Light (The Real Scientist Investigates)
Peter Riley, Sea-to-Sea Publications, 2011

Light and Sound (Sci-Hi)
Eve Hartman & Wendy Meshbesher, Raintree, 2010

Light and Sound (Essential Physical Science)
Louise & Richard Spilsbury, Raintree, 2014

WEBSITES

Watch this video to find out how rainbows form:
https://www.youtube.com/watch?v=vXccpwytjL8

Fun and informative science experiments about light:
http://www.exploratorium.edu/snacks/iconlight.html

This video explains how to create glow sticks:
https://www.youtube.com/watch?v=PZfHn1YJVGk

More hands-on experiments about light can be found here:
http://www.superchargedscience.com/documents/LightWave.pdf

GLOSSARY

angle shape made by two lines that meet at the same point

beam narrow strip of light

column tall, straight, solid piece of rock

convex shape that curves or bulges outwards

crystal special three-dimensional solid with flat sides and a regular shape

direction the way in which something or someone travels or faces

energy force or power

glare when light is so strong that it makes it difficult to see

goggles special glasses worn to protect the eyes

Inuit native people who live in parts of North America and Greenland

lens curved glass or plastic that makes things look bigger, smaller, and/or clearer

magnify to make things appear bigger

material type of substance

opaque something you cannot see through

prism something that separates light into its different colors

ray narrow line or beam of light

reflection light or an image that is bounced back off a surface

refraction the bending of light

retina part at the back of the eye that sends messages to the brain

shadow dark image on a surface, caused by an object blocking light rays

shimmer when something reflects light and quickly flashes

source where something first comes from

speed how far something moves in a given amount of time

translucent something that lets some, but not all, light through

transparent something that you can see through

INDEX